Finding
True North

Finding True North

Poems by
Janice Larson Braun

Published by
The Jackpine Writers' Bloc, Inc.

Published by The Jackpine Writers' Bloc, Inc.
13320 149th Ave, Menahga, MN 56464
sharrick1@wcta.net
www.jackpinewriters.com
Printed in the United States of America
Cover and book design by Tarah L. Wolff
Edited by Sharon Harris

ISBN: 978-1-928690-35-1

$10.00 USD

Grateful acknowledgment is made to the following
magazines and journals for the previous publication
of these poems:

Talking Stick 23: "The Gift," "This is your brain."
Talking Stick 24: "Aeolus," "The Keeper of Hope."
Talking Stick 25: "Family Dynamics," "It's Time."
Talking Stick 26: "The Next Morning," "Puppy Love."

Table of Contents

To Joe,
   my partner on the journey.

———————————

Finding True North

November

Minnesota mice are restless.
It is November, after all.
They have plans.
There is talk of California,
But the elders simply shake their heads—
It is time for a little B&E.

The cat and dog team swear they are ready,
Have been talking strategy
Since the first mishap.

And I,
As I listen to the roar
Of the wind in the Norway
And the din of leaden water
Clashing against the rocks,
I dread the coming carnage.
I am,
As my accountant points out each year,
Risk-averse.

This is your brain

This is your brain yesterday.
It hums with joy
At seeing names and dates and equations.
It purrs when you toss it words
Like "synecdoche" and "metonymy."
It feeds on data.

This is your brain today.
It is plumper and greyer
And not so interested in details.
It wades through the shallows
Of names and dates
With barely a fleeting glance.
It hums only as it slides
Into the deep pool of meaning,
Reflection,
And understanding.
Ask it what happened in 1066,
And it will shrug
And point to some murky weed bed
Over its shoulder.
But if you want to hear it purr,
Ask it why we don't learn from the past.
Or better still,
Ask it why people are so afraid of love.

The Call of the Wild

New snow this morning.
So the dog and I set out
To lay down a trail
To lay claim—to something.
Only deer and rabbits
Have gone before us.
Voyageurs! I think
Exploring the new world.

Flocks of mailboxes
Huddle together in the deep drifts,
Heads into the wind.
Steadfast spruce trees,
Spires reaching high into the heavens,
Kneel in quiet awe.

It is the beauty that stops us.
Or perhaps the truth—
Frozen whispers everywhere.
We are not alone in this wilderness.
Seek no more, it says.
Here is all.

The Gift

My daughter's gaze
Finds me across the room
As Christmas presents explode
All around us,
Wrapping paper drifting down,
Slowly covering the floor.
As the love from her smile
Melts into my pores,
All the shouts and giggles
Of generations
Simply disappear.
I feel the warmth traveling
Up my bones and into my chest—coalescing there
Where it circles a few times
Before lying down, content.
Where I will be able to hold it
In the certain cold months ahead,
Long after some plane
Takes her away.

Respite

Deep winter,
Sated and drowsy,
Settles around us
And inside us,
The stillness absolute—
No roaring winds,
No creaking trees,
No booming splinters of ice.
Just downy feathers of snow
Pillowing the rooftops
And filling up all our empty spaces.

And Mother Earth sleeps—
Burrowing into the deep quilt
Pulled up around her shoulders.
If she shifts in a warm dream
Of chattering squirrels
And giggling, sun-tickled blue water,
A quiet breath of wind
Sighs across the frozen lake.
Unconsciously she cradles her belly
While she dreams,
Protecting the seeds
Planted months before

And waiting.
As we all wait.
The chickadees will be the first to call—
Their solemn three-note whistle
Announcing to the world that morning breaks,
That spring will soon burst forth
In perfect squalling beauty.

Beneath the Surface

Today the little creek
That stoically battled against the bitter cold for months
Lost.
The thick, steel-grey water
Simply stopped.

Or so it seems
To the eye that only sees
A barren wasteland of snow and ice—
A tundra—
Where once a great lake lapped the shores.

But under that icy skin
Pumps life,
Fed by this little artery
That on this day
Healed shut on its own,
Leaving only the twisting turns
Of a pale white scar.

The Keeper of Hope

Sitting on the cold steel table
While strange fingers probe and needles sting,
Her eyes lock on mine,
Watching for a sign, a cue,
To tell her whether or not to let the fear in.
I am the one.

I am the keeper of all things—
    of the treats on the counter
    of the rules against jumping and biting and barking.
I am the keeper of the peace
    when the fuzzy little kitty stretches, yawns,
    and transforms into a yellow-eyed demon with claws.
I keep her safe—
    from skunks and cars and wood ticks
    and now, from cancerous tumors on the spleen.

But mostly I am the keeper of the heart.
And so, as I turn out the light
And we snuggle deeply into our pillows
And synchronize our breathing,
We slip into the night ahead
Together.

Walking Alone

Grief rolls over me,
Pounding, suffocating,
Swelling
Until I stagger under it.

Such grief does not tuck away
Into a purse or fanny pack
To be borne in secret,
So I hoist it up upon my back——
Shoulders balancing all that black weight
Eyes trained on the path ahead.
For what else can we do
But bear it?
Stooped with pain, I move forward
Day after day,
One foot after the other.

Waterlogged
I drift blindly across the bottom of the lake,
Looking for a quiet cove
Certain
I will never again float freely
In the dazzling light of day.

Transitions

All those famous painters
Who traveled to Venice to seek the perfect light
Ought to have come to Minnesota in February.

The sun gleams through trunks of white birch,
Spreading golden on the snowy hills,
Making all things new.

Even the old crusty snow—
    like some wrinkled tutu from childhood
    stuffed into the back of the closet,
    dusty and soft with old starch—
Glitters once again in this new light.

Perhaps it no longer dances in the wind
Or sparkles in the moonlight,
But it remembers
And dreams of diamond tiaras.

Neighbors

With his clear blue eyes
White, wispy hair
And thin stoop,
He is every old Norwegian
I have ever known.
We don't look at each other
As we talk,
Voices soft and melodic,
But gaze off into the safe distance
And flick glances at each other,
Timid smiles leaping back and forth.
And before I leave, a touch—
A firm squeeze on the arm
Names me "friend"
In both languages.
I miss my father.

Ode to the Mosquito

Every year I swear
I will learn to love you.
Gently I blow you away
From my still and patient arms.
I remind myself
That you are frail and delicate,
Gentle girls, just born,
And willing to face death
For those babes at home
Who depend on you to feed them.

But when I wake in the dark
To the steady drone
Of your nighttime sorties,
The war begins.
And my traitorous heart
Names you "enemy."
Even as I lie in wait
And plan my strike,
I remember—
The People name you
"Little spirit."

Lodestone

Evening.
The yellow sun melts and spreads
Across the satin water.
One pull of the paddle
And I glide forever—
Set free.
The edges of my blades
Slice into the silver coolness,
Sure, steady strokes,
Leaving whispering wrinkles in my wake.
As I always have,
I head true north—
A snow goose
Flying home.

Aeolus

Perhaps it is boredom
That causes the wind,
Restlessly pacing for days,
To gather itself
And spring into the sky with a roar.

It toys with the lake,
Lifting, dropping, rolling—
Hurling great sheets of water to splinter against the rocks
And dissolve into bits of foam.

Then it leaps up the hill between the stricken trees,
Flattening the grass,
And explodes at the crest with wild frenzy.

Gentler trees bend at the waist
And let their spines take the force of it.
But the young Norway pines cluster together,
Jostling each other with loud shouts,
Reveling in unleashed power—
Anxious for their turn to rule the world.

Grace

The storm has passed.
Wet leaves droop heavily
And pine trunks stand darkly
In the morning sun.
Disjointed branches and severed leaves
Lie strewn over the clipped grass.

And in the quiet coolness
We sit—
Shoulder to shoulder
At the end of the dock—
And watch the sun light up the opposite shore,
Content,
With the new puppy at our feet.

Love

The mother turkey pauses
At the edge of the road—
Listening, waiting—
And then proceeds to cross
In long, purposeful strides.
Behind her,
Swarming onto the road,
Surges her brood of little dustballs.
Skittering in every direction,
Chaos in motion,
They make it across the road
And disappear into the woods
Safe again.

The dog and I glance at each other
In shared joy.
He is grinning—
We know well this lesson
In trust and gentleness.

Lilies of the Water

Monet was right
About water lilies—
They glow softly,
These exotic heart-shaped leaves,
Green innocence
On the surface of the water—
Fluorescent as the sky darkens.

All summer long they lie there,
Quietly doing their work—
Cleaning the water,
Sheltering small fish,
Launching fleets of dragonflies.

Like a deck of cards they lie
Carelessly scattered
And still—
It only takes the right breeze
To set these hearts all aflutter.

Grounded

We were eighteen
The first time we stayed up late
Playing cards and giggling
Together.
Six of us
Alone on campus no longer.

Today, at sixty-five,
We cluster
Around the table—
Bright pink and yellow and blue hoodies
Glowing in the sun.
Coffee cups in hand,
Cards laid out in neat rows,
Laughter raining down,
We bloom again—
Playing solitaire
Together.

A Time to Every Purpose

One night,
For no apparent reason,
The weeds at the bottom of the lake
Simply let go.
I find them in the morning
When, coffee cup in hand,
I make my way
Down to the dock
To watch the day break
And to ponder the truths of the universe.

They float there,
These masses of long strands,
Still green
But no longer reaching for the sun.
It looks like death—
Like slaughter, in fact—
Unlike the birches on the hill
Who gleam in stately poses,
Gowns of golden yellow pooling at their feet.
There is no beauty here—
Even for one who waits and longs
For winter.

Savasana

Toasted leaves
Lie scattered on the forest floor
Baking in the sun
Like homemade bread,
Yeasty and warm.

One by one
They swan-dive down,
In perfect symmetrical arches
And submit—
Warriors no longer.

Vinyasa

The doe
On the hill
Stops grazing
To study me.
We learn each other.
She seems to be all neck
As she stretches up,
Ears cocked,
Waiting for my voice.

So I croon to her,
Telling her
What she already knows—
She is beautiful
And gentle
And beloved.

By Degrees

The sun has changed.
No longer
Do we feast on rich green leaves,
Deep orange and yellow nasturtiums,
Blood-red geraniums,
And soft blue lobelia.

Orange pine needles,
Just last week
Glowing warmly
On the path to the lake,
Lie dry and brittle—
Cooling
In the watery afternoon sun.
We will subsist
On stone soup
In the months ahead.

A Dog's Life

Those of us
With access to toilets
Will never, apparently,
Appreciate the finer points
Of the daily quest
To find the perfect poop spot.

I can tell you
It involves a great deal of
Trotting around the yard,
Repetitive circling
Over any potential site,
Regular scenting of the air,
And excruciating attention
To the details of plant life—
With an occasional nibble
At a delectable blade of grass,
Diversion or not.

Those of us,
However,
Who have tested
The parameters of love ourselves,
Cherish patience,
The stillness of hope,
And the shared joy of success.

Not Safe

The belly of the lake
Rumbles—
Hungry already
And winter just begun.

Late at night
Under the white moon
She groans and moans—
Giving birth
To new ice
That pushes its way
Into this world,
Fragile
But squalling.

With haunting calls
Of loneliness
She pulls at me.
Were I mermaid
Or silkie,
I would be gone.

As I Grow Older

Winter memories
Cluster together.
Like swans in open water
They float—
Tranquil and still—
So alike
I cannot name them.

They hover
In the late afternoon sun,
Reflections
As clear
And profound
As the memories themselves.

Sweet Sorrow

I wait poorly.
Counting helps,
So I count steps
From one window to the next.
I count almonds
That I feed the restless
Beast of anxiety.
I count sit-ups
That I do to stop eating almonds.

I count the seconds
That tick off the clock
And drift down steadily,
Filling the empty spaces
In the kitchen
Where I sit at the table
And play solitaire
And wait—
For that call
Which will tell me
You are home
And safe
And happy

And I can breathe.

Eden Redux

Old friends,
We gather at the table,
Coffee cups in hand,
And begin the ritual
Of passing the communal apples
And a paring knife
Around the table,
One to another.

Slicing off a piece,
We taste and eat,
Savor,
While our host tells us each apple's story—
Who, when and where it first grew—
A sacred history.

One at a time
We rediscover—
Tart or sweet,
Crisp or mellow—
Each gift of his labors,
The simple act of passing food
And sharing in his passion
Binding us together.

A Tragedy in One Act

MapQuest sends us blindly
From one road to another,
Four hours of black ribbons
Slowly unwinding before us,
Until a final maze of county roads
And roundabouts leads us
To a celebration of life
For an old friend
Whose own downward spiral
Was equally confusing
And precarious
And black
With only one way out.

Spring

What with
The constant hammering of woodpeckers,
The joyful honking of geese,
The bossy calls of the crows
Shouting directives from on high
And the muted chatter
All around,
It's official:
The crew has arrived
And construction season has begun.

A Lotus Flower

Petal by petal
Spring opens before us—
Sunlit patches of grass
Blush green,
Buds on branches
Lift their heads to the sky
And laugh out loud,
And soon
Soon
Summer will float
In lovely tranquility
Upon the open water.

Old Souls

I have walked this stretch of road
A thousand times—
Sometimes huddled in my parka
Against the January cold
That is steely and sharp-edged,
Sometimes dripping and panting
Under the July sun.
I know these trees
Along my path
And they know me.

This morning
We share the clear, sweet song
Of the flitting robin
And quietly remember
The relentless force
Of the northwest wind.
And something else we share—
Something quiet and true,
Something so elemental
It has no name.

Joie de vivre

In the drizzly rain,
The dog and I
Startle two deer
On the side of the road.
Their dainty hooves
Tap and skitter as they hit the pavement.
Then in two glorious bounds,
Like ballet dancers
Leaping onto the stage,
They are off the road
And disappearing,
Two white tails
Into the misty woods.

And I am reminded
Of tenth grade geometry,
My shiny silver compass
With its red stub pencil,
And the soaring joy
Of making perfect arcs
Everywhere.

Family Dynamics

Of all the seven sisters,
That Monday is the strict one.
She knows that Saturday and Sunday
And even Friday, if we are being honest,
Are pretty soft.
They encourage sloth in all its forms—
Sleeping late,
Eating oneself sick on Cheetos,
And lying on the couch
To watch hours of mindless television.
Tuesday, Wednesday and Thursday,
Born followers,
Passively do whatever they're told,
So Monday is stuck
Being the disciplinarian.

By the time she stands
At the front door,
Hands on hips,
Eyes in "I see you" mode,
Saturday and Sunday
Have slipped off for a nap,
And Friday, already distracted,
Hums to herself

As she practices
Some complicated dance step.
Tuesday-Wednesday-Thursday
Stand at attention
And watch as Monday
Points imperiously,
And we,
Heads bowed,
Shoulders drooping,
Plod out the door
And down the stairs
To face the week ahead.

Yoga Toes

Yoga has set my toes free.
They now grip carpet
And stretch out to their full length
And spread wide like turkey toes.

After years of being stuffed
Into dark cavernous shoes
And told to conform
To shapes not their own,
I am teaching them to think
For themselves
Independently.
Perhaps someday
They will learn to defy authority.

Revenge Served Cold

"The bears are hungry,"
I say over and over again
To console my friend
Whose bird feeders were demolished
By said bears.

In search of some noble truth,
I try to prod
Her empathy,
To awaken in her
The recognition that we must share
The earth's bounty,
And I say again,
"The bears are hungry."

But she smiles in satisfaction
At my pronouncement,
Content with their suffering,
With their hunger,
And announces
Loud enough
For the bears to hear,
In her sternest mother's voice,
"They should be glad
They're still alive."

The Dog Days of Despair

It is hard to be nice
In this heat.
My spirit,
Like some truculent child,
Wants to crouch
In the darkest corner
And ponder
All the injustices in the world,
To savor all the wrongs
Ever inflicted upon me,
Until Poor Me
Collapses in misery
And tears rain down,
Soothing and softening
The parched gentleness
Struggling to survive.

August

And already
My morning walk is streaked
With dark shadows—
Ominous fingers of the darkness
That is to come.

Undaunted
I wade into those
Cool black pools of mystery
Not yet illumined
By the mid-day sun,
For I know this path well
And do not fear
Possibilities
Born in the shadows
Of a new year.

It's Time

The sun is pulling away from us.
No longer white hot,
His light is pale,
His caress tepid.
Like some indifferent lover
Who just a few months ago
Warmed our beds at night
And brought us ecstasy every morning,
He now is distant.

He sits at my table,
Picking at his salad—
Fingers restless
Thoughts elsewhere.
He thinks about the hills of New Zealand,
The beaches of South Africa,
And something new and exotic
On the streets of Rio.

Finally, I fold my napkin carefully
On the table,
Look him directly in the eye
And ask,
"How long will you be gone?"

Semper Fidelis

I have fallen in love
With spruce trees.

Unlike the pines
Who dominate the landscape
Standing tall and full,
Grandly reaching arms up
In euphoria,
The spruce huddle quietly together
On the periphery,
Arms held shyly by their sides,
Taking up as little space as possible.

Pointed heads
Peek above the canopy
As they peer out at the world
In awe.

Coming Home

Like sweet young girls,
The waves smile at me
As they glide in
One by one
And break softly at my feet.

But out in the middle of the lake
Where they run wild,
They laugh out loud
With abandon—
Heads tossed back,
White teeth glinting
In the sun.

With Eyes Closed

In the black of night
I burrow
Into my husband's warmth.
His breath
Deep and steady
Laps over me,
Smoothing out
All the ragged
Edges of dreams,
His rolling snores
Rocking me to sleep.

Bleak December

Without blue
The world returns
To black and white.

The black road
Winds through the white snow
And the green-black pines.
Cold and bare,
The white birches
Raise arthritic fingers
To the grey-white sky.

All we can do is wait
For the advent of blue—
The color of hope.

Still, Still, Still

Daybreak in January
And alone I
Stand on the crest of the hill
And listen
To nothing.

There is no bird chatter
No lap of water on rocks
Not a breath of wind
Nor the sigh of leaves.

The earth rests
In downy sleep—
A soft hush
In deep quiet.

Just be.

Tuesday-Night Trivia

Once a week we gather—
Teams around tables
In circles of light,
Leaning in with gleaming smiles.
Anticipation hums

As we review details of this week's current events.
We shake the hoarfrost from our dendrites
And strike a spark for those old synapses.

Twenty questions—
Cars and quotes and Presidents and actors and athletes
All skim by,
But number ten—literature—
Is mine.

Taut, I await
The Bronte sisters,
Robert Frost,
Maybe James Joyce.
Tonight it is Elizabeth Barrett Browning,
And suddenly out of nowhere
A flash: *Sonnets of the Portuguese!*
I soar into the ether
Where I will float in glory
All week.

Absolute Zero

February shadows sprawl blue
Across the white snow.
The cold is deep
And still.

I tuck this image
Into memory
Where it rests—
At peace
With all I know to be true.

Matins

Early morning
And I sit on the dock—
Coffee cup in hand—
Watching the rising sun glow
Yellow on the tree tops
And glint
Silver on the glossy water.

I hear my name
And turn to see my sister,
Another early-riser,
Point to the hill behind me
Where sits a bear
Gazing out over the water,
At peace with the morning quiet
Hanging softly in the air.

I smile
And I swear it smiles back.
Then we each turn back
To the morning's slow arrival.

When I rise to go
The bear is gone,
The day begun.

Ice-out

When you live on a lake,
When you learn its changing moods,
It becomes a living thing.
It breathes—in and out,
Its pulse steady and even.

All winter it lies dormant,
Sleeping and silent
And still.
And you wait
Because you don't forget.
You breathe—in and out
And your blood pulses in your veins
And you watch and wait.

And then it happens—
Cracks form
Great sheets of ice shift,
And water surges
Free in the wind.

With tinkling bells
The ice floats away,
Honey-combed and fragile.
And the lake is back.

Spring Renaissance

Mist shimmers
In the morning sun,
As frog chatter
Pours from the swamp.
So much catching up to do:
    How was your winter?
    You look well-rested.
    I think you've lost weight again!
    How are the kids?
    Has anyone seen any flies yet?
And their little frog souls
Sing with joy.

Cooper vs. the Ducks

Every morning they face off—
Dog at the top of the hill,
Ducks waiting and watching from the lake.
All it takes is a squawk
And the pounding of wings on water
To set the dog in motion.

Two great leaps
Propel him down the hill
And launch him into the water.
Ducks scatter in his wake,
Alarm transforming to scolding
From a distance.

Dripping victory all the way up the hill,
The warrior dog marches past me,
Up the back stairs
And into the back hall
Where he waits stoically
For his morning toweling
And unmanly snuggle.

Burning Desire

In the still evening
When poplar leaves
Stop rustling
And just listen,
The oriole
Pours his joy
His exquisite love
Into all the empty spaces
Between the blue arching sky
And the green pulsing earth.

He knows life is tenuous
And we
Given but one chance
To glow
Orange and black
In the sunset.

Three Haiku

#1

Lacy lilac blooms—
Cotton candy on a stick,
All sweetness and light.

#2

Water lily buds
Bob gently at the surface—
Turtle heads breathing.

#3

Old Hoya blossoms
Once bright and full of promise
Now falling like tears.

Circles

Lying on my back in the sun,
I gaze at the endless blue
Of my childhood—

Waking to the hiss of the garden hose

The tang of the fresh-cut grass
Tickling my arms and legs

Sitting on a moss-covered rock
In the blueberry patch,
Smelling Labrador Tea
In the dappling sunlight

And my mother's voice.

An eagle circles slowly overhead.

Blessings from Heaven

Sun showers
My mother used to call them.
We would run inside,
Change into swimsuits
And spend the next twenty minutes
Dancing around the front yard,
Maniacs
Shrieking and laughing
As the cold drops slid down
Our sun-baked skin.

My brain still loves the paradox of sun showers
And my spirit the defiance
Of that adult pronouncement
That you can't have everything you want.

At Last

Welcome home,
North Wind.
I have been waiting for you—
Longing for you.

All business,
You scour out
The heavy, water-logged air
From every corner
Where it cowers and sulks.
With a brisk nod
You reenergize
The drooping birch
And maple trees
Who slough off their lethargy and rise.
And I—
I stand at the end of the dock
And embrace you.

August Again

And everything is fading.
Leaves and blades of green
Pale to yellow and brown,
Transitioning
From vibrant and superfluous
To dull and essential.

I sit alone on the dock
And grieve
The passing of time.
My daughter has gone back to Los Angeles.

The Fall

Leaves are falling.
Rain is falling.
Burnished yellow aspen leaves
Fall in waves
And stick to everything—
Like a child's sticky fingers
On the table
On my pants leg
On my cheek—
Fingers reaching,
Eyes beseeching.

Knowledge does not help.

True Love

My father loved home.
But he also loved my mother
Who wanted to see the world.
So every summer
He would get up before dawn
And drive us thousands of miles
So she could see starfish
And jellyfish
And deserts
And Texas oil wells
And mountains bloom purple on the horizon.
We saw the Lincoln Memorial
The Empire State Building
The Seattle Space Needle.

But on every trip
He reached a point
Known only to boomerangs.
Then, like an arrow loosed,
We arced true and clean
And headed home
To the Northwoods.

Puppy Love

Brutus has grown old—
Warm, chocolate eyes
Have become muddy,
His shiny black coat
Now coarse and grizzled.

I reach into the backseat
Of the pickup where he sits
To stroke his cheek.

He melts
Into my caress
And closes his eyes
When I lean in to kiss
His forehead.

The Next Morning

You wake up
And discover Sadness,
Small and grey,
Has burrowed its way
Into your heart.
Your eyes burn.

And in that spot
Just above your belly
Where you carry Hope,
There now lies
Coiled
And knotted
Something new and unnamed.

Into the Whiteness

I stand facing the frozen lake
And hear a lone bird call
And the moan of the lake making ice.
I swear I can hear
Each delicate snowflake
Free-falling from the sky
And landing precariously
On the icy crust of old snowbanks below.
I am ready for this new day.
I am ready.

Living In the Moment

Who would have thought
    in mid-March
I would need my parka—
    hood up—
The cold burning my thighs,
New, dry snow squeaking underfoot?

"You grow or you die,"
Says the Old Man.

After Spring Rain

The sun rises
On a world washed
Clean and green.
Buds become maple leaves,
Bird songs—
Loon and chickadee and phoebe—
Rise into the air,
Water surges, rising in the lake,
And in the softness of the morning light
My heart rises.

www.ingramcontent.com/pod-product-compliance
Lightning Source LLC
Chambersburg PA
CBHW060421050426
42449CB00009B/2066